Learning about
the Church

by Felicity Henderson
Illustrated by Michael Grimsdale

A LION BOOK

Copyright © 1984 Lion Publishing

Published by
Lion Publishing Corporation
10885 Textile Road, Belleville, Michigan 48111, USA
ISBN 0 85648 525 X (casebound)

First edition 1984
Reprinted 1984

Text by Felicity Henderson
Illustrations by Michael Grimsdale

Printed and bound in Italy by
Imago Publishing Ltd

There are followers of Jesus all over the world.
They live in different countries and
speak different languages.
But they all belong to God's family because
they follow Jesus.

There are friends of Jesus in every country.
They live in cities, towns and villages.
In some places they meet in a house,
but usually they meet in a church.

It might look like this,

or this,

or this,

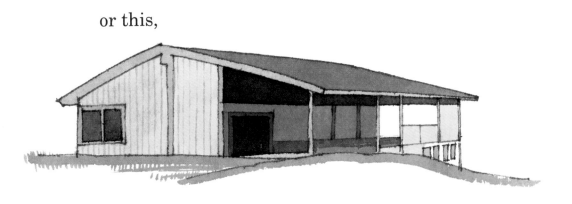

or this.

A church is where God's family meets together.

Some churches are big. Some are small.
Some are very old. Some are new.
They are all different.
But the most important thing about a church
is the people.

They are all different too –
babies, little children, boys, girls,
moms, dads, old people – all God's family.
They all love God, and they believe in Jesus.
God is like a father to them.

Sunday is the special day when people go to church.
In church they say a special family prayer
together, the prayer that Jesus taught.

'Our Father in heaven,
May your name be honored,
May your kingdom come,
May your will be done on earth
as it is in heaven.
Give us today the food we need.
Forgive us the wrongs we have done,
as we forgive others
the wrongs they have done to us.
Do not bring us to the test,
but keep us safe from evil.
Amen'

Some people kneel
to pray in church.

Some people sit.

Some people stand.

But they are all talking to the same God.
They are all friends of Jesus.

Jesus is God's son.
He came to live in our world a long time ago.
He showed people what God is like
by the things he did and said.

'Follow me,' he said to his friends.
That means to be like Jesus,
and to do as he says.

Jesus prayed to God his father.
So we can pray too.
We can thank God for his goodness and
ask him to help us and other people too.

Jesus and his friends sang songs to God.
So we can sing to God too –
psalms and hymns, songs and choruses.

Jesus and his friends read the Bible.
So we can read it too.
The Bible tells us about God's love
and the good news about Jesus.

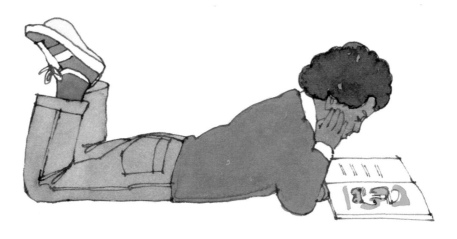

Jesus talked to his friends about God.
We can learn about God too.

Do you have cards and presents on your birthday?
Birthdays are special days in every family.
Christmas is special for God's family
because it is Jesus' birthday.
We send cards and presents to one another.
We thank God for sending Jesus to live
in our world.

The Bible says, 'God loved the world so much
that he gave his only Son. And whoever believes
in Jesus will not die, but have a new life,
for ever.'

Easter is another special day for God's family.
On Good Friday people remember how Jesus
died on the cross.
The Bible says, 'Jesus Christ died once and
for all, to bring us back to God.'

But the most exciting thing of all is that
after three days Jesus was alive again!
That is what people remember on Easter Sunday.
It means that anyone who loves and follows
Jesus need not be afraid of dying.

In church on Sundays – and other days too –
people meet together to praise God, to read
the Bible, and to learn more about him.

In a special service, people eat a piece of bread and drink a sip of wine. This is to remind them that Jesus died for them, and that we need Jesus as much as we need our daily food.

When someone believes in Jesus and
follows him, he becomes part of God's family.
Jesus said, 'Tell everyone about me, and
baptize everyone who believes in me.'
'Baptism' is a sign of God's promise to
forgive us and to give us new life.
The first followers of Jesus were baptized
in a river. This still happens in hot countries.

In cooler countries grown-ups are baptized
in a special pool inside the church.
In many countries babies are baptized.
They do not go into the water, but they
are sprinkled with water.
The parents promise to teach the child to
follow Jesus until he is old enough to
be 'confirmed'.

So God's people meet together
in church on Sunday.
They are a family – God's family.
They belong together.

In most churches there are special
ministers (sometimes called a vicar, or priest
or pastor) who give their whole lives to
helping and teaching people in the church.
But everyone in the church has an
important job to do.

They want to help each other,
　　and to love each other,
　　and look after each other.
And they want to tell other people about Jesus.

But they are not just God's family
on Sundays.

They are God's people on Monday, Tuesday,
Wednesday, Thursday, Friday and Saturday too.

Today there are followers of Jesus all over the world.

They live in different countries and speak different languages.

But they all belong to God's family
because they follow Jesus.

Learning about the Church – special words

Baptism – a service which takes place
when someone decides to become a follower
of Jesus. Different churches have different
customs. When someone goes into the water,
or is sprinkled with water, it is a sign
that God has forgiven their sins and they
are 'washed clean'. It is the beginning of
a new life with God.

Confirmation – in churches where babies are
baptized, the parents and God-parents
promise to bring up the child to follow
Jesus. When he is old enough, and decides
to follow Jesus, he 'confirms' these promises
in a special confirmation service.

Christian – the name given to a follower
of Jesus.

Communion, Lord's Supper, Mass, Eucharist –
different names for the same service using
bread and wine. This reminds Christians
of the Last Supper, and the death and
resurrection of Jesus.

Resurrection – when Jesus rose from the
dead.

Look up these stories in the Bible

The first Christmas –
Luke 2:1–20

Jesus chooses his disciples –
Matthew 4:18–22

The Last Supper –
Matthew 26:26–30

The first Easter –
Matthew 28:1–10

The Bible verse on page 17 is from John's
Gospel 3:16.

The Bible verse on page 19 is from The
First Letter of Peter 3:18.